CHRISTMAS KIDCHAT

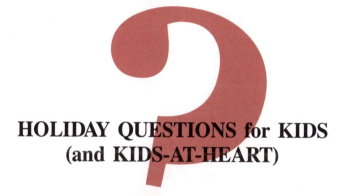

HOLIDAY QUESTIONS for KIDS (and KIDS-AT-HEART)

Bret Nicholaus and Paul Lowrie
The Question Guys™
Authors of the national bestseller
The Christmas Conversation Piece

QUESTMARC Publishing,
a division of QUESTMARC Entertainment

QUESTMARC

Entertainment / Publishing
P.O. Box 340
Yankton, SD 57078

© **2002 Bret Nicholaus and Paul Lowrie**

Illustrations by Scott Luken
(P.O. Box 159 • Yankton, SD 57078)

Cover and text design by Donna Bollich
and Mary Ann Hoebelheinrich

ATTENTION: SCHOOLS AND BUSINESSES

Questmarc books are available at quantity discounts with bulk
purchase for educational, business, or promotional use.
For more information, contact:
Questmarc Publishing, Special Sales Department,
P.O. Box 340, Yankton, South Dakota 57078.

ISBN #0-9634251-7-X

Printed in the United States of America

First Edition: September 2002

10 9 8 7 6 5 4 3 2 1

For Grant,
with all my love

Bret

For all the inspiring kids
I've met along the way

Paul

WELCOME

First of all, thank you for taking a few moments to pick up our book; we appreciate the opportunity to tell you what this project is all about. Much like *KidChat*, our original children's question book, this thought-provoking collection of questions was written to get kids thinking creatively and talking enthusiastically—in this case, about anything and everything related to the holiday season. We cover every Christmastime topic you can possibly imagine and more! From candy canes to Christmas cookies, old St. Nick to newly fallen snow, gift-giving to gift-receiving, it's all right here in *Christmas KidChat*.

Kids will absolutely love this book from the moment they first open it up, as it will lead them into exciting holiday conversations that they've never had before. They'll have a blast using the book with their peers, but they'll also discover that the book works great with their parents. In fact, one of the best times to use this book is at family gatherings during the holidays. Kids will enjoy picking out a question and asking it to the group...and before you know it, everyone from Mom and Dad to Cousin Eddie is involved in a fun and lively discussion. Of course, *Christmas KidChat* is ideal for any type of Christmas party where kids are part of the mix, and it's a great way for children to pass the time on those long holiday trips in the car or on the plane. And don't forget the classroom opportunities it affords: Teachers regularly use these questions as creative writing stimulators and as a tool to get students talking about a wide variety of holiday topics.

Since there is no particular order to the questions, kids can open to any one of the 200 questions and start right there. There are no wrong answers to these questions—only opinions. Often times, kids will discover that the way they think changes from day to day; the answer given for a question today may be completely different from their answer to the same question tomorrow—and that's perfectly fine.

Regardless of whether this book is used in the car, in the classroom, or just sitting on the couch with friends or family members, kids will have hours and oodles of fun providing spontaneous answers to the entertaining questions contained in the book. And as for all of you adults out there? Well, let's just say that we have a strong suspicion that your children won't be the only ones enjoying *Christmas KidChat* this holiday season!

Happy conversations to all,
Bret Nicholaus and Paul Lowrie

Special Note
Throughout this book, kids will periodically notice a heading that says "Imagination Igniter." These words indicate that the question below it is specially designed to stimulate very creative thinking and the "full-blown" use of their imagination.

"Imagination is more important than knowledge."

—Albert Einstein

1

If you could wake up on Christmas morning to see snow falling in any color, what color would you want the snow to be?

2

If you could take one tradition from another holiday and somehow make it a part of the Christmas season, what tradition would you choose?

IMAGINATION IGNITER

3

If you were asked to create an all-new, never-before-seen toy that would be sold to kids all over the world, what would this new toy be called and what would it do?

4

If you could spend your winter break anywhere in the world, where would you want to go?

5

What Christmas song more than any other do you look forward to hearing every holiday season?

6

S uppose that you could receive only one Christmas gift this year, and that one gift had to begin with the letter P. What gift that begins with this letter would you want most of all?

7

If you could change the natural scent of Christmas trees from pine to anything else, what new scent would Christmas trees have?

8

What is the best Christmas gift you've ever received?

9

What is your favorite thing to do to help your mom or dad get ready for Christmas?

IMAGINATION IGNITER

10

If a local bakery asked you to create an all-new Christmas cookie, putting into it any ingredients that you wanted, what would this new cookie be like?

11

If something besides snow could fall from the sky on Christmas Day, what would you want it to be? Assume that there would be no mess or safety issues to think about. (Example: Fresh strawberries.)

12

This Christmas, would you rather receive just one large gift (in terms of size) or five *small* gifts?

13

If you had to spend this holiday season living in any unusually large or famous building, what building would be your home for the holidays?

14

Suppose that you could decorate your entire neighborhood with Christmas lights, but all the lights had to be the same color. What color would you want the lights to be?

15

If, for one day during winter break, you and your friends could have any one place completely to yourselves, what place would you choose? (Example: The local movie theater.)

16

If you could change one thing about the way Santa Claus looks, what change would you make?

17

If snow could fall in any fruit flavor, what flavor would you choose?

18

What is your favorite Christmas movie or holiday TV special to watch each year?

IMAGINATION IGNITER

19

If you could build a toboggan slide for your neighborhood, what would you do to make the slide really cool and fun?

20

If you could have played the part of any character from a holiday movie or play, who would you have wanted to be?

21

If you were helping Santa Claus deliver toys to the children all around the world, what country (besides your own) do you think would be the most fun to visit on Christmas Eve?

IMAGINATION IGNITER

22

If you were asked to design a brand-new sleigh for Santa to ride in, what particular features would you be sure to include on the sleigh? (If you make the new sleigh large enough, you could even include a small swimming pool!)

23

What is the most fun Christmas-related event you've ever been a part of or attended?

24

What is your favorite part of decorating the Christmas tree? (Examples: Arranging the lights, putting on the ornaments, hanging candy canes, placing the star at the top, etc.)

25

If you were in charge of making a really cool gingerbread house for your school classroom, what type of candy or other treat would you use for the roof?

26

Thanksgiving (and the holiday season in general) is the time of year when people remember all that they have to be thankful for. What are you most thankful for this year?

27

What is your favorite food that appears each year on the Thanksgiving Day table?

28

What is one Thanksgiving food your mom or dad likes to eat that you don't like at all?

29

If you were going to buy your best friend a Christmas gift this year, what gift do you think he or she would like more than anything else?

30

What musical instrument do you think of first when it comes to Christmas?

IMAGINATION IGNITER

31

If you were a king or queen and had to deliver a Christmas proclamation to all the people in your kingdom, what Christmas message would you give them?

32

If you could receive any one intangible gift this year (in other words, a gift you can't physically touch with your hands), what would you want most of all? (Examples: An extra week off of school, no bedtime for the holiday season, the freedom to eat all the Christmas sweets you want, etc.)

33

What person in your family do you have the most fun shopping for during the holidays?

34

What is the most unusual Christmas gift you've ever bought or made for someone?

35

Do you think it's fun to watch other people open gifts that you have bought for them? Why or why not?

36

If you could have it your way, how many inches of snow would you like to wake up and find on the ground on Christmas morning?

37

If you could spend this Christmas in any one of our 50 states besides the one in which you live, which state would you most want to visit this holiday season?

38

Would you rather spend this Christmas out in the country on a farm or in a big, busy city with really tall buildings? Why?

IMAGINATION IGNITER

39

If you could throw a huge Christmas party at a hospital for sick children, what specific things might you do to make it a Christmas the kids would never forget?

40

If you could choose any animal other than reindeer to pull Santa's sleigh, what type of animal would you pick?

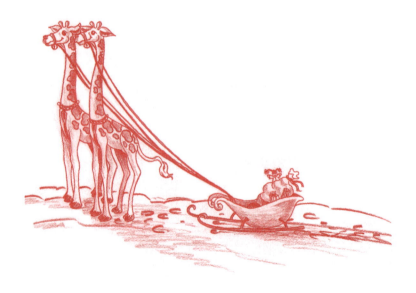

41

What is one particular toy out there that you wish would go away and never come back?

42

Have you ever asked any elderly relatives about what Christmas was like when they were kids? If you've never asked them, you should; you just might find their answers very interesting.

Have you ever shaken a wrapped present to try and figure out what was inside? Have you ever snuck around the house, looking in closets or under the bed, trying to find out what Christmas presents your parents have bought for you? If so, have you ever gotten caught?

What is one really fun activity you did last Christmas that you hope you can do again this Christmas?

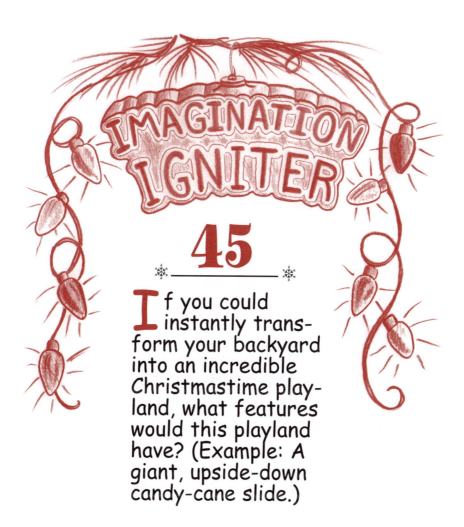

IMAGINATION IGNITER

45

If you could instantly transform your backyard into an incredible Christmastime playland, what features would this playland have? (Example: A giant, upside-down candy-cane slide.)

46

Does your family have any holiday traditions? If so, what tradition is your favorite? Why?

47

Based on what you know of the biblical Christmas story, what character do you think is the most interesting? Why?

48

If you could make one change to a popular toy that would make that toy even better than it already is, what toy would it be and what specific changes would you make?

49

If you could have 50 pounds of anything you wanted this Christmas, what would you choose?

50

What is your favorite ornament that hangs each year on your family's Christmas tree?

51

If an angel suddenly appeared in front of you, do you think you would be scared or filled with joy? Why?

52

If you were asked to draw an angel as you think one might look, how would you draw it? Why do you think an angel might look like that?

Which would you rather have this Christmas season: a three-foot-tall candy cane or three gallons of hot chocolate?

If you could invite anyone in the world to spend Christmas with you and your family, whom would you invite?

Have you ever gone Christmas caroling? If so, what part of it was the most fun?

IMAGINATION IGNITER

56

Have you ever stopped to think about what Christmas must have been like for kids who were living 100 years ago? What do you think some of the big differences would have been? What are some things that might have been similar back then to the way they are now?

33

57

If someone gave you $100 in cash as a Christmas gift, what do you think you would do with the money?

58

In terms of actual size, what is the smallest thing that you really want this Christmas?

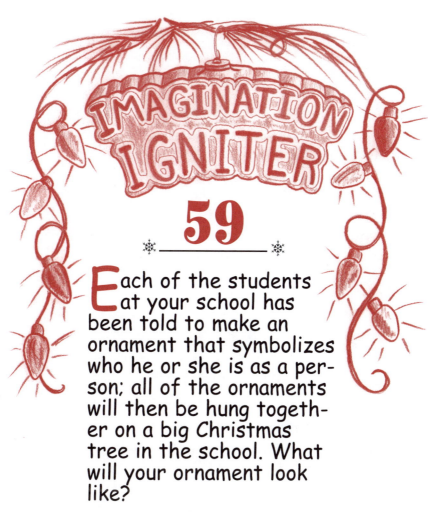

IMAGINATION IGNITER

59

Each of the students at your school has been told to make an ornament that symbolizes who he or she is as a person; all of the ornaments will then be hung together on a big Christmas tree in the school. What will your ornament look like?

60

If you have a pet, is there anything special you do for it during the Christmas season? What new thing could you do for it this year?

If you don't have a pet, what is something you think you would do at Christmas if you *did* have a pet?

61

If you were asked to create your own personal design or pattern for wrapping paper, what would this wrapping paper look like?

62

If you could start a tradition where something other than ornaments would hang on Christmas trees around the country, what would you choose to hang in place of ornaments?

63

How tall do you imagine that the average elf is?

64

If you could ask one question to any person in the biblical Christmas story, to whom would you ask the question and what would your question be?

65

If you could jump into a time machine and travel back in history to see any Christmas from long ago, what Christmas celebration do you think would be fun to see?

66

If it were completely eliminated from the holiday season, what Christmastime food or sweet would you miss the most?

IMAGINATION IGNITER

67

If you were creating a movie about toys coming to life, which toy would be your main character and what would its name be?

68

What is the funniest thing that has ever happened to you or another family member at Christmastime?

69

If, as a Christmas gift, you could have any wish come true, what wish would it be?

If you were invited to be a special guest in a big Christmas parade and in the parade you could ride in any vehicle of your choice, what would you choose to ride in?

If a bunch of your friends were coming over to your house for a Christmas party, what would you want to eat and what would you do to make it a really fun party?

42

72

Have you and your family ever cut down you own Christmas tree? If not, do you think it would be fun to do sometime? Why or why not?

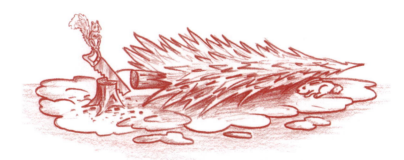

73

Do you think it's more fun to spend Christmas at your own house or travel somewhere else for the holidays?

74

If you could have a basketball-sized snow globe with any scene inside, what scene would you want?

IMAGINATION IGNITER

75

If Santa asked for your help in naming three new elves that had come to work in the toyshop, what names would you give them?

76

Suppose that your winter break from school could be two weeks longer than it is, but that in exchange your summer break from school would be two weeks shorter. How would you feel about this arrangement?

77

What is the best Christmas gift your mom has ever received? What is the best Christmas gift your dad has ever received? (If you don't know, just ask them.)

78

What was a typical Christmas like for your mom when she was growing up? What was a typical Christmas like for your dad when he was growing up? (Again, if you don't know the answer, ask them.)

79

What do you think is the most fun thing to do with your friends when you are on winter break from school?

80

On a scale of one to ten, with one being you don't mind waiting at all and ten being you can hardly wait another minute, how impatient do you get when it comes to having to wait until Christmas to open up your presents?

81

What are three specific things about the Christmas season that you really like? What are three things about the Christmas season that you don't like so much?

IMAGINATION IGNITER

82

If a Christmas card company asked you to draw a Christmas picture that would be put on the front of thousands of Christmas cards, what would the picture or scene be?

83

Which do you like more and why: the week before Christmas or the week after Christmas?

84

How many different animals can you think of that have something to do with the Christmas season? (Think of songs, stories, holiday traditions, etc.)

85

Besides Christmas, what is your favorite holiday of the year? Why?

86

If you could see any Christmas exhibit of your choice at a large museum, what exhibit would you want to see?

87

If you were going to a school Christmas party where everyone had to dress up in a holiday costume, what or whom would you dress like?

88

Do you think Christmastime will be more fun or less fun when you are an adult? Why?

IMAGINATION IGNITER

89

If you were asked to write a Christmas book that would be sold in bookstores throughout the country, what would your story be about?

90

Who is someone you know that might be feeling a little sad at this time of the year? What could you do during the holidays to make this person feel happier?

91

What do you imagine that Santa likes to do in his free time, when he's not busy delivering toys or helping his elves at the workshop?

92

What is one job that you think would be really fun to have during the holidays?

93

Which of your friends from school do you miss seeing the most when you are on winter break? Which teacher do you miss the most?

94

What is your favorite thing about the Christmas season that begins with the letter M?

IMAGINATION IGNITER

95

If you could create a new, special candy just for the holiday season, what would this sugary sensation be like and what would you call it?

96

If an alien from another planet arrived in America knowing absolutely nothing about the celebration of Christmas, what particular aspect of the holidays would you want this outer-space visitor to see or experience? What aspect of the holiday season do you think this alien would find the most strange?

97

What is your favorite holiday commercial on TV this year?

98

If all your Christmas gifts this year had to come from the same store, which store would you choose?

99

What are some holiday traditions or ethnic customs that your friends and their families have that differ from your own family's traditions? Which of their traditions do you think would be fun to try in your own family?

100

If you were Santa Claus, what food (and drink) would you want kids to leave for you on Christmas Eve?

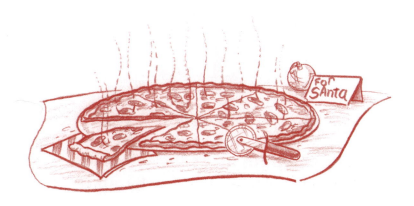

101

※———————※

What is your all-time-favorite scene from a Christmas movie?

102

※———————※

If you were the governor of your state, what is one really special thing you would do at Christmastime for the people who live in the state?

IMAGINATION IGNITER

103

If your mom or dad would let you decorate the front door of your house any way you wanted, how would you decorate it?

104

If you could choose anyone except Santa Claus or yourself to be the grand marshal of a holiday parade in your town, whom would you choose to lead the parade?

105

Do you like to make your own Christmas gifts for people in your family or do you prefer to go out to the stores and buy them? Why?

106

Besides the Christmas tree, what is your favorite decoration that your mom or dad puts out in the house every year at Christmas?

107

If you could change one thing about Christmas, what change would you make? (It can be a change that affects everyone around the country or it can be a change that only affects you or your family.)

108

Not counting Rudolph, which of the other eight reindeer do you think has the coolest name? (Choices: Dasher, Dancer, Prancer, Vixen, Comet, Cupid, Donner or Blitzen.)

109

We all know that Santa's favorite snack is milk and cookies, but what about Rudolph? What do you think is the favorite snack of the world's most famous reindeer?

110

Would you be willing to give up all of your Christmas gifts this year in exchange for one year of peace throughout the entire world? Why or why not?

IMAGINATION IGNITER

111

What Christmas object do you think would best symbolize your personality? (Example: A candy cane if you are a really "sweet" kid.)

112

If you could decorate a tree for another holiday besides Christmas, what holiday would it be and how would you decorate the tree?

113

If somebody asked you where in the Bible they could find the best account of the Christmas story, would you know where to tell them to look? (If you don't know, the answer is in small type at the end of question #132.)

114

In your family, what is the most important aspect or element of Christmas? Do your friends and their families celebrate the holiday season for the same reason/s you do?

115

At what point in the year do you usually start to think about the Christmas season? (One of the authors of this book begins to think about it right after the Fourth of July!)

116

If you were an elf in charge of building toys, what toy above all others would you want to help make?

117

What is usually the first thing you and your family do to kick-off the holiday season each year?

IMAGINATION IGNITER

118

If your mom or dad asked you to pick something red, something green, and something white to eat for a Christmastime meal, what three foods would you choose to put on your plate?

119

What is your favorite thing to do around the family Christmas tree?

120

What is the tallest decorated Christmas tree you've ever seen?

121

Does your family open most of its gifts on Christmas Eve or Christmas Day? What about your friends' families?

122

There are three wrapped gifts under the Christmas tree, and you may choose only one. One gift is pyramid-shaped, one is circular, and one is square (they are all about the same size). Without being allowed to pick them up or shake them, which shape would you want?

123

If you could make a telephone call to wish a "Merry Christmas" to anyone in the world, whom would you dial up?

124

If, as one of your gifts this year, you could get an autograph of anyone in the world, whose signature would you want most of all?

125

What is the most trouble you've ever had finding or getting a Christmas gift for someone?

126

What do you think is the most enjoyable thing to do in the snow?

127

If you were riding with Santa in his sleigh up in the sky, what do you think would be the coolest thing to look down and see?

74

IMAGINATION IGNITER

128

If you could develop a roller-coaster ride with Christmas as its theme, what would the ride be like and what would you name it?

129

Would you rather receive one (and only one) very large and very expensive gift on Christmas Day, or a very small and much less expensive gift every day from December 1st through December 25th? Why?

130

If you could go sliding down a really high and steep hill but had to do it on or in something out of the ordinary, what would you choose for your speedy trip down the hill? (Example: The mattress from your bed.)

131

What is the latest you've ever stayed up on Christmas Eve?

132

What is one really nice thing you could do for your parents this holiday season? Go ahead and do it!

The answer to question #113 is Luke 2:1-20.

133

If you were given 1,000 candy canes, what do you think you would do with all of the striped sweets?

IMAGINATION IGNITER

134

If you were invited to write a Christmas article for your city's newspaper, what holiday subject would you choose to write about and what would the headline say?

135

Do you think Christmas would be as much fun if it were celebrated during the middle of summer? Why or why not?

136

What is the funniest Christmas joke you can remember?

137

If you could take a train ride any-where you wanted this Christmas, where would you want to take this holiday ride?

138

If you could "jump into" the words of any Christmas song and actually experience everything that's happening in that song, what Christmas song would you choose?

139

If you could have any place in the world iced-over so that you and your friends could go ice-skating there, where would you choose? (Example: If you love baseball, maybe Yankee Stadium.)

140

If you could help decorate for the holidays any store in your area, what store would you choose?

141

If your birthday could fall on the same day as any holiday, which holiday would you choose? What would be the advantages and disadvantages of having your birthday on the same day as the holiday you chose?

IMAGINATION IGNITER

142

If you were a Christmas tree, how would you want to be decorated for the holidays?

143

During the Christmas season, what is something you and your parents could do together each night at the dinner table that would make dinnertime more interesting and fun for everyone?

144

If you had to rank the following holidays/special days in order from your favorite to your least favorite, how would you rank them? (Choices: Valentine's Day, the last day of school (which is also the first day of summer break), the Fourth of July, Halloween, Thanksgiving, Christmas, and your birthday.)

145

Have you ever played with a toy so much right after Christmas that within a few days you were tired of it? If so, what was the toy?

146

How many different people or characters from the biblical Christmas story can you recall from memory?

IMAGINATION IGNITER

147

If you could create your own original character for a Christmas program at school, what type of character would you be up on stage?

148

As a kid, what is something about the holiday season that seems odd or strange to you? (In other words, what is something you just "don't get" about this whole Christmas thing?)

149

What is something you always used to love to do at Christmastime that, during the last couple of years or so, you feel like you've "outgrown" or lost interest in doing?

150

Besides receiving presents, what is one aspect or feature of Christmas that you wish would last all year long?

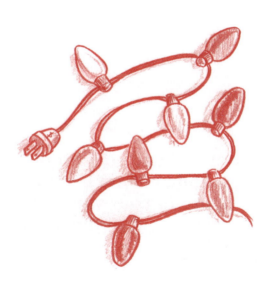

151

If you could spend the holidays with any family from a TV show or movie you like, what family would you choose?

152

If there were a huge amount of snow on the ground and you had to build a snow sculpture in your yard, what would you create out of the snow? (No snowmen, please.)

153

If you had to fill a large TV-sized box with brand-new toys for a kid whose parents couldn't afford to buy him or her any Christmas presents, what type of things would you put in the box?

154

Of all your relatives that live far away, which one do you most wish could come and visit you this Christmas?

155

If Christmas could be celebrated twice a year, at what other time of the year would you want to celebrate it?

156

If, for the holiday season only, you could convince your parents to change or eliminate one rule that they've set for you, what rule would it be?

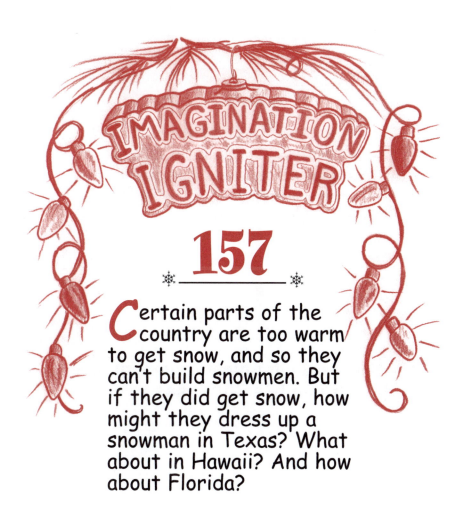

IMAGINATION IGNITER

157

❄ ——————— ❄

Certain parts of the country are too warm to get snow, and so they can't build snowmen. But if they did get snow, how might they dress up a snowman in Texas? What about in Hawaii? And how about Florida?

158

Besides those of the United States, what country's Christmas customs and traditions are you most interested in learning about?

159

What is the funniest ornament on your family's Christmas tree?

IMAGINATION IGNITER

160

If a company that makes breakfast cereal asked you to create a holiday cereal that would be sold to kids throughout the month of December, what would the cereal be like?

161

What do you imagine that the Christmas star that shone over Bethlehem looked like?

162

What is your favorite Christmas sound?

163

He's making a list and checking it twice…. On a scale of one to ten, with one being very naughty and ten being extremely nice, how naughty or nice have you been this year?

164

What relative's house do you most like to visit during the holiday season?

165

If you could choose any one day of the year—regardless of the season—to have six inches of snow fall, what day would you choose? (Examples: Your birthday, the last day of school when summer break begins, the Fourth of July, etc.)

166

If you could go to a holiday concert starring any musical artist or band of your choice, whose concert would you want to attend?

IMAGINATION IGNITER

167

If you could create a brand-new instrument for the holiday season, what would it look like and how would it sound?

168

The two main colors of Christmas are green and red. If you could choose two new colors to represent Christmas, which two would you pick? Why?

169

Spring, summer, fall and winter—always in that order...but what if you could change that? If you could rearrange the order of the four seasons any way you wanted, what would the new order be?

170

If you could convince Santa Claus to move his offices from the North Pole to any other location in the world, to what new place would you want him to move?

171

If you had lots of your own money and could buy your mom anything at all this Christmas, what would you buy for her? What would you buy for your dad?

172

If you could bring to life any character from a Christmas book, who would it be?

173

What is your mom's favorite Christmas memory from when she was a kid? What is your dad's favorite Christmas memory from when he was a kid? (As always, ask if you don't know.)

174

When Christmas is over, is it more fun for you to see what your friends got as gifts or to show them the gifts that *you* got?

IMAGINATION IGNITER

175

If the United States Postal Service asked you to design a new holiday-season stamp, what would this new stamp look like?

176

If, for the Christmas issue, you could have your picture on the front cover of any magazine, what magazine would you choose?

177

What is your favorite catalog to look at during the holidays?

178

Have you and your family ever been stranded anywhere during the holidays because of bad weather? If so, where? For how long?

179

What is the best Christmas party you've ever been to?

180

What is one activity you really wish you could do right now but can't because it's December? (Example: If you're in a cold climate, swimming in an outdoor pool.)

181

If you had to go the entire month of December without something you really like, what would you find the most difficult to give up for these 31 days?

IMAGINATION IGNITER

182

If you had to pick something other than a sleigh for Santa to travel around in on Christmas Eve, what would you choose? Be creative! (Example: A speed boat.)

183

Has there ever been a gift you really wanted but your parents wouldn't buy for you? What was their reason for not buying it?

184

What is the longest distance you've ever traveled in order to be with other family members for the holidays? (If you're not sure, ask your parents.)

185

Sometimes, kids will get a little puppy or kitten as a Christmas gift. If you could receive for a Christmas gift any baby animal of your choice, what type of animal would you choose? Assume you would have the space and proper means to care for it.

186

As a Christmas gift, would you rather receive $250 in cash (to spend however you want) or a vacation with your family to Walt Disney World?

187

Is there any particular thing that you've always wanted to do during the holidays but as yet have not done? If so, what is it?

188

Have you ever been in a Christmas play? If so, what part/s did you play?

189

Would you rather spend Christmas high up in the mountains somewhere or on a sunny island out in the ocean? Why?

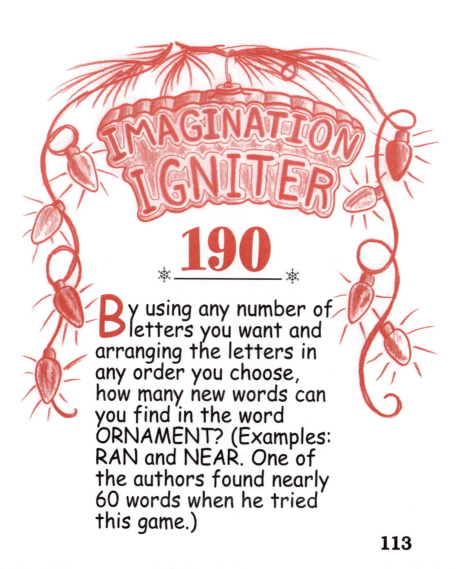

IMAGINATION IGNITER

190

By using any number of letters you want and arranging the letters in any order you choose, how many new words can you find in the word ORNAMENT? (Examples: RAN and NEAR. One of the authors found nearly 60 words when he tried this game.)

191

Can you think of any particular holiday food (including any cookies) that your mom or dad makes that you really don't like?

192

In your opinion, what one object best symbolizes what Christmas is all about?

193

What is the latest you've ever stayed up on New Year's Eve?

194

Over the course of this last year, what do you believe is the most important lesson you've learned?

195

What is the most exciting thing you did this year?

196

More than anything else, what are you looking forward to doing in the coming year?

197

In the year ahead, what is one thing you think you'll get a lot better at than you are right now?

IMAGINATION IGNITER

198

If you could print on a highway billboard any holiday message you wanted—a message that would be seen by thousands of people driving by—what would your large sign say?

199

If you could do anything you wanted—
anything at all—on New Year's Day,
what would you do?

200

If you could add your own original
holiday question to this book, what
would the question be?

Got a question of your own that you'd like to send us? How about giving us your answer to one or more of the questions in this book? We'd love to hear from you. Write us a letter, put it in the mail, and we'll be sure to get it...as long as you address it as follows:

Bret and Paul, The Question Guys™
P.O. Box 340
Yankton, South Dakota 57078

Thanks for taking the time to write us, and always keep asking questions!

About the Authors

Bret Nicholaus and Paul Lowrie, The Question Guys™, are the authors of a dozen question books, including the highly popular children's book *KidChat*. Altogether, they have written over 3,200 questions and sold nearly 500,000 copies of their question books. While this is their second book of holiday questions (*The Christmas Conversation Piece* came out in 1996), this is the first one written specifically with kids in mind. Nicholaus and his family live in the Chicago area; Lowrie makes his home in Yankton, South Dakota.